Other 'crazy' gigglebooks by Bill Stott
Sex – it drives us crazy!
Marriage – it drives us crazy!
Football – it drives us crazy!
Cats – they drive us crazy!

Published simultaneously in 2004 by Helen Exley Giftbooks in Great Britain, and Helen Exley Giftbooks LLC in the USA

12 11 10 9 8 7

Selection and arrangement copyright © 2004 Helen Exley
Cartoons copyright © 2004 Bill Stott
Design by <rog@monkeyboydesign.co.uk>

ISBN 978-1-86187-757-4

Printed in China

Helen Exley Giftbooks, 16 Chalk Hill, Watford, Herts, WD19 4BG, UK
www.helenexleygiftbooks.com

A HELEN EXLEY
GIGGLEBOOK

Rugby

IT DRIVES US CRAZY!

CARTOONS BY BILL STOTT

"The ball!
I caught the ball!"

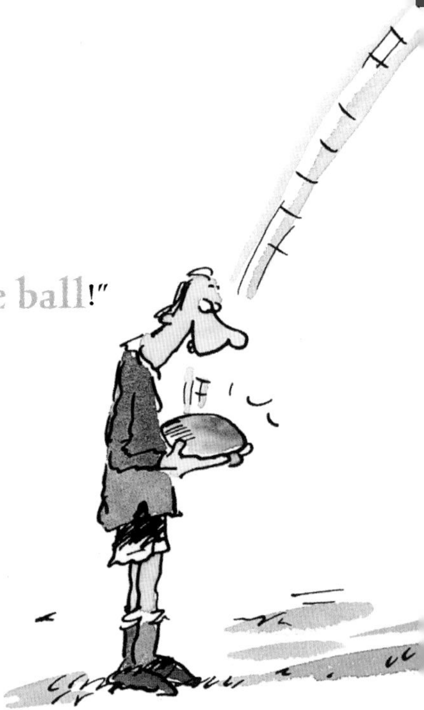

"And anybody going anywhere
near their flanker should have
private medical insurance..."

"I saw that – you swallowed my whistle!"

"School rugby? It's done wonders for his character but not a lot for his teeth."

"Not releasing the ball Ref?
He can't release the ball."

1 "Wait".

2

"I think I lost a lens."

"Go on Ref, don't call it off.
Our forwards hate it too firm..."

"Great horned tortoiseshell
or not – kick the ball!"

"What do you mean, I'll look better with all my teeth in? These are all I have!"

"Get that dog into a shirt and a pair of shorts and we're in with a chance."

"You called him a big girl. That's a sexist
remark. Sin bin. Ten minutes!"

"No, no – Auntie Doreen isn't hurting Daddy... Auntie Doreen is playing against Daddy..."

"He was hoping to turn out for the vets this week, but he fell off a bar stool."

"We can't find your teeth, but here are a few nobody claimed last week."

"Ooh! I've got Handel's Messiah on my radio."

"Two and a half minutes.
That's some clearance!"

"So, Gary, a 98-3 thrashing. Disappointed?"

"French referees usually have some quirky ideas about rule interpretation."

"You're quite right, I did play rugby.
How did you guess?"

"Teeth, glasses, hairpiece –
sure you've taken everything off?"

"Did I stick my thumb in his eye? Only by mistake – I was aiming for his ear!"

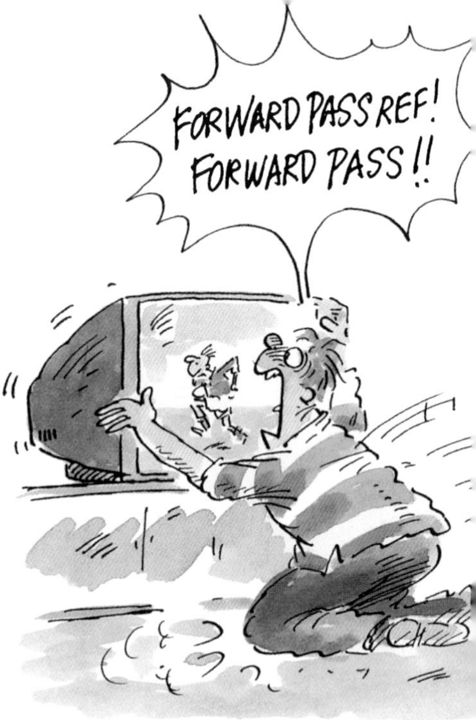
FORWARD PASS REF!
FORWARD PASS!!
CHRIS

"The TV's not that interactive, Darling."

"Chauvinist?
Don't be silly –
shut up and give us a kiss..."

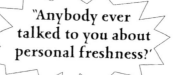

"You think they play badly?
Wait till you hear them sing!"

"And in the fifth team, youth and maturity are united by one common factor – total lack of ability!"

"Go on – he called you a rude name – then what?"

RULE 528: "A good big 'un always beats..."

1

"... a good little 'un."

"Well played – whoever you are!"

"When you're 6'6" and 300lbs, no one minds if you wear a shower cap."

"Actually, he was hoping you'd send him off then he could go home and watch the international..."

"Lovely run – beautiful dummy, but you can't score tries with their number seven's boot..."

"There he was – way offside, so I naturally looked around for you – to draw your attention to the infringement. You were nowhere to be seen."

1

"So I floored him."

"Nice try – no ball – but nice try!"

"I hate rugby, but I love rolling in mud."

"For heaven's sake – what now?"

"I know we do this every week because we love it, but can you think of any reasons a sane person would understand?"

"Did you win, then?"

About Bill Stott

Bill Stott is a freelance cartoonist whose work never fails to pinpoint the absurd and simply daft moments in our daily lives. Originally Head of Arts faculty at a city high school, Bill launched himself as a freelance cartoonist in 1976. With sales of 2.8 million books with Helen Exley Giftbooks, Bill has an impressive portfolio of 26 published titles, including his very successful *Spread of Over 40's Jokes* and *Triumph of Over 50's Jokes*.

Bill's work appears in many publications and magazines, ranging from the *The Times Educational Supplement* to *Practical Poultry*. An acclaimed after-dinner speaker, Bill subjects his audience to a generous helping of his wit and wisdom, illustrated with cartoons drawn deftly on the spot!

What is a Helen Exley giftbook?

We hope you enjoy *Rugby – it drives us crazy!*. It's just one of many hilarious cartoon books available from Helen Exley Giftbooks, all of which make special gifts. We try our best to bring you the funniest jokes because we want every book we publish to be great to give, great to receive.

HELEN EXLEY GIFTBOOKS creates gifts for all special occasions – not just birthdays, anniversaries, weddings and Christmas, but for those times when you just want to say 'thanks' or 'I love you'. Why not visit our website, www. helenexleygiftbooks.com, and browse through all our present ideas?

ALSO BY BILL STOTT
Marriage – it drives us crazy!
Cats – they drive us crazy!
Football – it drives us crazy!
Sex – it drives us crazy!

Information on all our titles is also available from
Helen Exley Giftbooks, 16 Chalk Hill, Watford WD19 4BG, UK. Tel 01923 250505